1833 STATE CENSUS

for

BARBOUR COUNTY, ALABAMA

Copied by Helen S. Foley

Southern Historical Press, Inc.
Greenville, South Carolina

Please direct all correspondence and orders to:

www.southernhistoricalpress.com
or
SOUTHERN HISTORICAL PRESS, Inc.
PO BOX 1267
375 West Broad Street
Greenville, SC   29601
southernhistoricalpress@gmail.com

ISBN #0-89308-177-9

Printed in the United States of America

Foreword

From Alabama History & Archives:

Acts of Alabama, No. 53 - That in 1833 a census was to be taken of each county in Alabama, using the following form:

Column 1 - White Males under 21
Column 2 - White Males over 21
Column 3 - White Females under 21
Column 4 - White Females over 21
Column 5 - Total amount of Whites
Column 6 - Total amount of Slaves
Column 7 - Total amount of Free people of Color
Column 8 - Total amount of inhabitants

Two copies were to be sent to the Secretary of state and one copy was to be kept by the clerk of the county court. This is copy of the original found in the office of the probate judge of Barbour County, Alabama. Some names were illegible.

Notes on the 1833 Barbour County Census

Baker, Larkis (Larkin) - Warren was a younger brother -
    Robert was a son of James Baker, Sr.

Bass, Josiah - buried at Bass Cemetery, Barbour County.

Battel, Culin (Cullin Battle) was a deacon at Antioch Baptist
    Church.

Benton, Sarah - was mother of Isaac and Wright - see Samuel
    Benton's estate 1834.

Blanket, Henry - Blanchet in 1840 Barbour census.

Butts, Charles - buried near Texasville. Married a Flournoy
    when middle age.

Canady - Kennedy

Carsey, Lemuel (Casey) buried at Ozark, Ala.

Currie, Cary - was a Primitive Baptist preacher. His name
    appears in Warren Co., Ga. records.

Dill, Robert, born in New England. He was married three times,
    once to Delilah, dau. of Jesse Ricks, whose will is in
    Pike Co., Ala.

Euford - Efurd

Flernoi - Flournoy

Gormon, John - one John Gormon of Edgefield Dist., S. C.,
    names heirs Nancy Kirksey and Rhoda , wife of Bud
    (Budd, family name) Bledsoe. Rhoda is buried at Union
    Church, 16 miles west of Union Springs, Ala.

Green, John - one John Green was from Edgefield Dist., S. C.,
    his father was Jacob Green.

Griggars, Stephen - should be Driggers

Hartsoz, David - children listed were not his - their
    father had recently died.

Helms - from Anson Co., N. C. - sons lived Dale & Coffee
    Counties in Ala.

Holom, Moses - there was a Moses Helms.

King, Wm., wife Polly was a sister of Larkin Baker.

Lee, Lovard - brother to Needham Lee, not same family as
    Timothy Lee.

McGilbery - McGilvary

Minsey - Minshew

Perswell - was Purswell in 1840 Barbour Census .

Parmer, Jared - married Martha Stripling in Jones Co., Ga.,
    in 1812. Vet. of War of 1812 - daus. married Robert
    and Timothy Lee.

Ryan, Hampton - is buried at Jack   Hightower's place near
    Clayton, Ala.

Stinson, Micager - name appears in Pike Co., Ala., estate
    papers.

Thomas, Joel - son-in-law of Peter Hagler.
    " , Morton,   "   "   "   "
    " , Tristram - his wife was a McIntyre.

West, Alfred - was a Methodist preacher - buried at Pond
    Bethel in Barbour County.

Williams, B. C. - (Bartley) - Pulaski Co., Ga.
    " , Buckner - Hancock Co., Ga., his brother was a judge.
    " , Sterling & Emanuel Cox married sisters.

1833 CENSUS BARBOUR COUNTY, ALABAMA

James Black	2	1	2	1	6	2	8
W. T. Long		1			1		1
James Nichols		1			1		1
G. J. Cole		1	2	1	4	9	13
Hugh Currie		1			1		1
Robt. Daniel		1			1		1
Thomas Lampley	1	1		2	2		4
D. J. Cole		1			1		1
W. G. Filyeaw		1			1		1
O. J. Williams	2	1	1	1	5	1	6
James L. Simkins		1	1		2	1	3
Alfred Elmore		1		1	2		2
H. J. Doyle	1	1	1		3		3
J. N. Bunkley	1	1	1		3		3
Grady Bearfield	1	1	1		3		3
W. R. Ladd		1			1		1
Ann Chaney	1		1	1	3		3
Triston Dolton		1			1		1
B. W. Goodson	1	1	1	1	4	5	9
Abslom Harper	3	1	3	1	8		8
D. B. Reder	1	1		1	3	1	4
Joel Simes	3	1	4	1	9		9
Richard Gary	1	1	1	1	4		4
H. W. Baker		1			1		1
John Tailor		1			1		1

Name	A	B	C	D	E	F	G	H
T. H. Thomas		1	1		2	1		3
John Jackson	1	1	1		3	3		6
John Bailey		1	1	1	3			3
W. B. Cole		1			1			1
James Clarke	2	1	3	2	8	10		18
B. T. Pilly	1	2	1		4	1		5
G. W. Underwood	1	1		1	3			3
Owen Lewis		1			1			1
Nancy Miller	1			1	2			2
Thomas Gray	5	1		1	7	7		14
William Arington	2	2	3	1	8			8
James Teringson	5	1	1	1	8	3		11
Seth Mabery		1			1			1
Samuel Powell		1		1	2			2
Josiah Thomas		1			1			1
Francis Johns		1			1	5		6
Timothy Johnson	7	1	1	1	10			10
Duncan McCrary	5	3		2	10	1	1	12
William Cloyd		1			1			1
H. F. Bizzel	1	1	4	1	6			6
W. H. Ayrz	3	1	1	1	6			6
Nathan Joiner	3	1	3	1	8			8
Seth Bennett	1	1	1	1	4			4
Ivy Warren	1	1	1		3			3
J. P. Hood	1	1		1	3		5	8

Daniel Hood		1	4		5		5
John C. Cole		1			1		1
William Bowden	5	1	4	1	11		11
G. J. Loveless		1	1	1	3		3
J. G. Coleman	1	1	2	1	5	5	10
John T. Martain		1			1		1
Alen Holme	2	1	1	1	5	10	15
Thomas Bobbet		1	3	1	5		5
G. W. Jackson	2	1		1	4		4
W. A. Tharpe	3	2	1		6		6
George Rolain	4	1	5	1	11		11
Robt. Gibbins	4	1	5	1	11		11
Isham Ivins		1			1		1
Redmon Benett	3	1	2	1	7		7
G. W. Horton		1	3		4	1	5
Philip Johnson	4	1	3	1	9		9
Jesse B. Colmon		1			1		1
Wm. Reder		1	3		4	3	7
Blake Justice	2	1		1	4	1	5
W. S. Hancock	1	1	1	1	4	1	5
James Bass		1	1		2		2
Moses Brigman	3	1	4	1	9		9
Partrick Ham		1			1		1
Josiah Harelson	1	1		1	3		3
William Dickson	3	1	3	1	8		8

Wm. Grubs	3	1	2	1	7	9		16
Josiah Bass	2	1	3	1	7			7
Robt. McCall		1			1			1
W. J. Sephens	1	1	3	1	6			6
Thomas Griggs		1			1			1
William McCormack		1			1			1
Jesse Ham		1			1			1
J. W. Edge	4	1	2	1	8	2		10
Hartwell Ball	1	2		1	4	8	1	13
T. E. Nesbit		1			1			1
Hansel Bird		1	1		2			2
J. M. N. McClain	1	1	1		3			3
Alexandria Kelley	1	1	1	1	4			4
S. A. Kersey		1	2		3	1		4
Henry Jerry (?)	1	1	1		3			3
William Dorman	2	1	2	1	6			6
William Cooper	1	2	2		5	15		20
B. R. Hood		1			1			1
John Ledbetter	1	3	1	2	7			7
Samuel Tindal		1			1			1
Jepthe Night	2	1	3	1	7			7
John Gormon	1	1	2	1	5	1		6
J. S. Williams	3	1	1	1	6	10		16
Edward Hering		1			1	1		2
W. J. Armstrong	4	1	1	1	7			7

J. B. Armstrong		1			1		1
Alfred Pugh		1			1		1
George Garvis		1			1		1
John Skipper	2	1	1	1	5		5
Hugh McClain		1			1		1
Henry Stokes	2	1	1	1	5		5
James Lasetor	2	1	3	1	7		7
Stephen Lasetor	1	1		1	3		3
George Gooden		1			1		1
Henry Grady		1			1		1
William Shaw		1	1		2		2
Martain McClendon	2	1	1	1	5		5
Joseph Morris		1			1		1
Jesse Newton	3	1	4	1	9		9
David Watson		1	1	1	3		3
T. C. Euford	4	1	2	1	8	14	22
P. H. Balldee	1	1	2	1	5		5
Henry Anderson	1	1	1		3		3
Milton McDonald	1	1	2	2	6		6
John Williams	1	1	1		3		3
William Black	1	1	4	1	7		7
Aaron Helms		1	1		2		2
William Wadkins	1	1	1		3		3
William Largins	2	1		1	4		4
Elias Marshal		1			1		1

Lewis Williams	2	1	1		4		4
Lewis Guy (Gray?)	2	1	4	1	8		8
John McClain	1	1	3	1	6		6
Lewis Valentine		1			1		1
John Green (?)	1	1	1		3	1	4
John Duglass		1			1	12	13
J. J. Burlison	2	1	1	1	5		5
David Tanzy		1			1		1
John Slone	1	1	1		3	4	7
Neal Norton		1			1		1
William Adkinson	3	1	2	1	7		7
W. S. Smith		1		1	2		2
Jerry Leggar (?)	2	1	4	1	8		8
John Ivy	1	1	2		4	4	8
Andrew Bass	2	1	2	1	6		6
J. W. Stricklin		1			1		1
Abraham Helums		2	1	1	4		4
Middleton Brooks		3	3	1	7		7
William Laird	1	1	1	1	4		4
Edmon Wiggans	2	1	2	2	7		7
A. J. Cox	1	1	1		3		3
Nathan Zitros	2	1	4	1	8		8
Isham Dansby		1	2		3	7	10
Hicks Cain	4	1		1	6		6
Daniel Griset	2	1	2	1	6		6

Name	C1	C2	C3	C4	C5	C6	C7
Hugh McCall		1			1		1
Bayford Fearcloth	3	1	2	1	7		7
Morton Thomas	3	1	3	1	8		8
Charles Long	2	1	1	1	5		5
Rinza Dorman (?)	5	1		1	7		7
Samuel Hays		1	1	1	3		3
Jordan Aullman		1	1		2		2
Kinson Tailor	4	1	5	1	11		11
John Farrior		1			1	2	3
Petter McClendon	1	1	5	1	8	3	11
James Shipman	6	1	3	2	12	5	17
Thomas McElvin	2	2		1	5	9	14
John Vann	2	1	3	2	8		8
James Wilkerson	1	1		1	3		3
Curtis Bizzel	1	1		1	3	4	7
John Westbrook	3	1	5	2	11	5	16
Lewis Lancester	3	1	3	1	8		8
James Stephenson		1			1		1
James Norton		1			1		1
W. G. Wilkerson		1			1		1
Arba Hering		2	1		3	13	16
R. Cambel	1	1		1	3		3
Archabold McKnabb	1	1	1		3		3
John Cuningam		1			1		1
G. Lewis		1			1		1

Emanuel Cox	3	1	2	1	7	13	20
Seaborn Lewis		1	4	1	6	14	20
John Alstin	3	1	3	1	8	7	15
Benjamin Sellers	3	1	3	3	10	2	12
Petter Highland		1		1	2		2
Beauford Foster		1		1	2		2
John Octon		1		1	2		2
Joel Helum	3	1	4	3	11		11
D. B. McDonald	2	1	6	1	10		10
Bryant Farior	3	2	3	1	9	1	10
Daniel McDonald	3	1	3	1	8		8
David Ketchum	3	1	4	1	9		9
Adam Grubs	3	1	2	1	7	16	23
Henry Faulk, Jr.	3	1	6	1	11		11
Hilrey Newman	3	1	3	1	8		8
Daniel McKenzy	1	1	1		3	33	36
Edward Cox		1		1	2		2
William Terel		1			1		1
Larkis Baker	3	1	2	1	7		7
James Cole	1	1	2		4	5	9
Abner Cambel	2	1	2	1	6		6
Samuel Bell		1			1		1
Nathaniel Holms		1		1	2	1	3
Jacob Utsey	4	1	3	1	9	15	24
Willson Collins	3	1	3	1	8	8	16

Hardy Helms		1			1		1
Jacob Minsey	1	1	2	1	5		5
George Gilman		1	1	1	3		3
W. S. Shanks	5	1	2	1	9		9
Isaac Teat		1			1		1
James Faulk	2	1		2	5	22	27
Samuel Lovat		1			1		1
Denis Bryant	2	1	2	1	6		6
Samuel Simkins	2	1	2	1	6		6
Rynal Gillis	1	1		1	3		3
John McKinis	2	1		1	4		4
Edward Bird	.	1		1	2		2
Angush Currie	4	1	3		8	8	16
Jesse Cox		1	2	1	4		4
Hector McKinis	2	1	2	1	6		6
Malcom Nair		1			1		1
H. L. Faulk		1			1		1
Daniel Curie		1	1	1	3	7	10
John W. Jackson	4	1	1	1	7	17	24
Moses Harelson	1	1	3	1	6		6
John Bizzel		1	2		3		3
Lewis Creal	6	1	2	2	11		11
Jeremiah Waren	1	1		1	3		3
Cary Cradler	1	1	2	1	5		5
J. H. Edins	1	1	1		3		3

(Casey?)

Lemuel Carsey	1	1		1	3			3
John Garner	1	1	3	1	5			5
Elias Bass	2	1		1	4			4
John Thomas	3	1	5	1	10			10
A. W. Faulk		1	2	1	4	1		5
Thomas Hobdy	4	2	1		7	1		8
Hinchy Green	1	1	3	1	6	11		17
Bradford Long		1	1	1	3			3
William Beasley	4	1	1	1	7			7
Littleton Glass	1	1	1		3			3
John H. Anderson	3	1	1	1	6	1		7
Grady Herring		1		1	2	11	1	14
Willis Flowers	2	1	1	1	5			5
White Pynes	1	1		1	3			3
Alen Johnson	2	1	1	1	5	1		6
Denis Condrie	1	1	1	1	4			4
David Farrior	1	1	2	1	5			5
Jasmith Jackson	5	1	2	1	9	27		36
Rody Eidson	3		2	1	6	1		7
George Stinson	3	2	1		6	7		13
Buckner Williams	1	1	2	1	5			5
Hinton Rivenbacher	1	1	1	1	4	5		9
Abner Flowers	5	1	3	1	10	4		14
James Baxley	4	1	2	2	9			9
Henry Hargraves		1	2	1	4	3		7

David Lester	2	1	3	1	7	3		10
G. B. Wheeler	4	3	1	1	9	4		13
Green Beauchamp	1	1	2	1	5	4		9
Edward Warren	1	1	3	1	6	20		26
Mason Dorman	2	1	2	1	6			6
E. A. Warren	1	1	1	1	4			4
Elisha Skiner	3	1	3	1	8			8
William Morrison(?)	5	1	2	1	9			9
Aaron Berlison	3	1		1	5	4	1	10
James Beasley	1	1	2	1	5	8		13
Hamton Ryan	4	1	2	2	9	8		17
Willis White		1	3	1	5	1		6
John Miller	3	1	1		5	21		26
David Spear	4	1	3	1	9	10		19
Tolbot Bell		1			1			1
W. C. Gibson	2	1	1	2	6	1		7
Robt. Martain	5	1	2	1	9	13		22
Samuel V. Langenham		2	3	1	6			6
Mathew Valentine	2	1	4	2	9			9
J. H. Morison		2	2	1	5	33		38
Hamton Thomas		1			1			1
J. Bigford	1	1	2	1	5			5
Sharevick Stutz	1	1	2	1	5			5
Counsel Williams	1	1	2	1	5			5
William Williamson	2	1	2	1	6			6

John Simons	2	1	2	1	6		6
Baker Adams	2	1	1	1	5		5
Anguish McCloud	1	2		1	4		4
Nathan Horn		1	1	1	3		3
John Musgrove	2	1	4	1	8	2	10
James Wilks	2	1	3	1	7		7
Charles Beasley	4	1		1	6		6
M. E. Bush	4	2	7	2	15	2	17
J. R. Norton	1	1		1	3	1	4
Asa Kirkland	3	1	1	1	6		6
W. J. Glass		1			1		1
Hamilton Rachaels		1			1		1
George Bachels	2	1	1		4		4
William Newman	1	1	2		4		4
William Brown		1			1		1
T. J. Watley	3	1	1	1	6		6
Seaborn Daniel		1			1		1
Petter Carn		1			1		1
Edwin Pulin	1	1	1		3		3
Samuel Canady		1			1		1
W. C. Creach		1			1	10	11
Edward Perdue		1			1		1
James Carol		1			1		1
Aaron Powel	2	1	2	1	6		6
Samuel J. Smith	5	1	1	1	8	12	20

Neal McRae	2	1	2	1	6	10	16
James Larry		1			1		1
Neham (?) Bryant		1			1		1
J. A. Wellborn		1			1		1
Riley Huland		1	3	2	6		6
George Gillmore	1	1	3	1	6		6
Hosey Baily	3	1		1	5		5
John Powel	1	1	4	1	7		7
Henry Pagget	2	1	3	1	7	2	9
Daniel McClendon		1			1		1
G. W. Whikker		1	1		2		2
E. L. Ott		1			1	19	20
David Wimberley	3	1	3	1	8	8	16
Charles Sutton	5	1	4	1	11	7	18
S. McClain		1		1	2		2
D. S. Steward		1			1		1
J. S. Faulk	2	1		1	4		4
Ucal Cunningham	1	1	1	1	4		4
Benjamin Franklin		1			1		1
Goren Norris	1	1	1	1	4		4
G. Benson	1	2	3	1	7		7
Alen Lovett	2	1	3	1	7		7
James Grayham	1	1		1	3	2	5
W. C. Grayham	2		1		3		3
Alexandria Steward		1	1	1	3	2	5

John Steward		1		2	3	3	6
J. A. Morris		1			1		1
William Alums		1	4	1	6		6
J. S. Steward	1	1	2	1	5	1	6
Stephen Smith	1	1		1	3		3
Wm. Bryant		1			1		1
William Harrison	1	1		1	3		3
John Davis	5	1	2	1	9	2	11
G. S. Davis		1			1		1
Western Whitier	1	1	2	1	5		5
Thomas Faulk	1	1	1	1	4		4
Duncan Cunningham	4	1	4	1	10		10
M. A. McMelon		1	2	2	5	9	14
Henry Hall		1			1		1
Daniel Hall		1			1		1
Duncan Fulton	1	2	4	2	9	1	10
A. D. McRae	4	1	3	2	10		10
John Tindal	3	1	3	1	8	2	10
Anguish Fergeson	1	1	2	1	8	4	12
John Read	2	1	2	2	7		7
E. B. Linzy	2	1	1	1	5	1	6
James Robeson		1		1	2		2
D. K. Thomas	2	1	1	1	5	1	6
Zachariah Thomas	1	1	2	1	5	2	7
D. McCloud	3	1	1	1	6	1	7

Edward Eidson	3	1		1	5		5
W. H. Hardy(?)		1			1		1
T. S. Orgain(?)		1			1		1
Henry Brown		1	3	1	5		5
Jacob Linzy		1	1	1	3	1	4
David Jernigin	2	1		1	4		4
Daniel Lincler	2	1		1	4		4
Valentine Brewer		1	2	1	4		4
James Smith		1	1	1	3		3
William Owens	1	1	1		3		3
Avry Nolain	1	1	2	1	5		5
Thomas Kent	6	1	1	1	9		9
J. M. Ivins	2	1		1	4	1	5
William Johns		1			1		1
Leroy Gunter	1	1	2	1	5		5
Thomas Canady	2	1	1	1	5		5
John Holin(?)		1	3	1	5	3	8
T. G. Kent	1	1	1		3		3
Joel Winslit	3	1	2	1	7		7
Andrew Killingsworth		1		1	2		2
Daniel Gilis	3	1	1	1	6		6
F. S. Jackson		1			1	3	4
Watts Mann	3	1	2	1	7	3	10
Robt. Mann		1		1	2		2
Jesse Holden	1	1	1	1	4		4

William Henry		1			1		1
Hilman Thompson		1	2	1	4		4
Redin Rullin	1	1	1	1	4		4
F. E. Sanders	2	2	3	1	8	1	9
A. D. Cooper	3	1	3	1	8	1	9
Jehew Wilkisson		1			1		1
J. C. Jackson		1			1		1
Bayfor Fulgem	2	1	2	1	6		6
James Wall	1	1	3	1	6		6
William B. Adam	1	1	2	1	5		5
Benjamin Filugan	3	1	5	1	10		10
David Berlemey(?)	4	1	1	1	7		7
John Elis	6	1		1	8		8
Mathew Fenn	2	1	1	1	5	8	13
John R. Jackson	1		1		2		2
Hardy Brown		1			1		1
Joseph Mincey	4	1	4	1	10		10
Simson Row		1			1		1
Jesse Johnson	2	1	4	1	8		8
Abraham Shiver		1			1		1
Terry Preswood	1	1			2		2
W. H. Gought(?)	2	1	2	1	6		6
William Gormon		1	2		3	7	10
R. C. McSwain	3	1	4	2	10	14	24
Elisha Arington	1	1	1	1	4		4

Robt. Hobdy	2	2	1	1	6	14	1	21
Burris Waren	2	2	4	1	9	17		26
S. C. Bradley	2	1	2	1	6			6
John Eidson	2	1	2	1	6			6
S. F. McMury	3	1	4	1	9	3		12
Eliot Thomas	3	1	2	1	7	10		17
William Gandy	6	1	2	1	13			13
Daniel Hughs		1	1	1	3			3
Levi Price	3	1	2	1	7			7
R. S. McMury		1			1			1
William Holman	2	1	1	2	6			6
James Clemons	3	1	1	1	6			6
Ryan Benet	1	1	1		3	1		4
A. D. Berlison	1	1	2	1	5			5
Fair Pynes	3	1	1	1	6			6
T. J. Warren		1	2		3	3		6
Elisha Hancock		1	1		2			2
Thomas Blakey		1		1	2			2
Michael Currie		1			1			1
Willis Bell	1	1	1	1	4			4
William Davis	4	1	2	1	8			8
Wiley Hines		1		1	2			2
Duncan McRae		1			1			1
J. B. Grambery	1	1	2	2	6	4		10
George Powell	3	1	2	1	7			7

D. G. Phincy		1		1	2		2
G. B. Keener		1	1	1	3	9	12
Phelex Johnson		1			1		1
Elva Lewis	1	1	2	1	5	15	20
James Prewit	2	1	1	1	5		5
Samuel Hall		1	1	1	3		3
Buck Bush		1			1		1
John Grant	1	1	3	1	6	1	7
Jesse Blakey	1	3			4	5	9
Roderick Ryan		1			1		1
West Herring	2	1	3	1	7	4	11
R. A. Sharp (Tharp?)	3	1	6	1	11		11
Bethel Burton		1	1	1	3	1	4
James Motley	1	1	4	1	7		7
Solomon Buttes		1	1	1	3		3
J. R. Norton	6	1	4	1	12	3	15
W. H. Gansy	2	1	1	1	5		5
Samuel Slaughter		1			1		1
J. R. Vickers	3	2	2	1	8		8
John McMelon		1	1	1	3		3
David Scarborought		1	2	1	4		4
Franklin Anglin	1	1	1	1	4	12	16
John Bell		1	1	1	3	2	5
W. V. Norton		1	4	1	6	3	9
Richard Cotton	1	2	1	1	5		5

T. B. Vickers		1	1		2		2
Ichabod Herring	1	1	1	1	4	1	5
Moses Williams		1	1	1	3		3
Jacob Shiver		1	1		2		2
William Hinson	2	1		1	4		4
Alexandria Johnson	1	1	1		3		3
Right Benton		1			1		1
Turner Ivins	1	1	2	1	5		5
T. S. White	3	2	4	1	10		10
G. B. Powel		1	1		2		2
Willey Squires	2	1	1	1	5		5
Emory Day		1			1		1
Barney Rouse		1	1	1	3		3
Stephen Hart	3	1	3	2	9		9
John Graham		1			1		1
James Bowden	4	1	2	1	8		8
S. W. Blakey		1		1	2		2
C. G. Brantley		1		1	2		2
W. H. Kilpartrick	3	1	3	1	8		8
William Blair	2	1	1	1	5	2	7
John Smith		1			1		1
W. F. Stephens		1			1		1
Ivy Herring	1	1	3	1	6	4	10
Theophilus Floid	2	3	3		8		8
J. E. John	2	1		1	4		4

Alexandria McClain		1			1		1
Samuel Lewis		1	2	1	4		4
J. W. Samuels	3	1		1	5		5
Thomas Holmon		1			1		1
Waren Baker		1			1		1
John Roads	1	2		1	4		4
Henry Neace		1			1		1
David Neace		1			1		1
Charles Lewis	3	1	4	2	10	2	12
J. H. White		2	1	1	4	18	22
Thomas Waren	2	1	1	2	6	26	32
John Peyton	5	1	3	1	10		10
John Hall	1	1	1		3		3
J. M. Dunn	1	1	1		3		3
Warric(?) Kilpartrick		1			1		1
Amos Lewis	5	1	3	1	10	6	16
Isham Fealder	5	1	5	1	12		12
Pulaski Mann		1	2	1	4		4
Robt. Deshazo	1	1	1	1	4		4
J. E. Deshazo		1	1		2		2
T. B. Keiner	3	1	2	1	7	7	14
Archabold McIntosh	6	1		1	8		8
E. V. Laningham	5	1	4	1	11	7	18
William Neace		1	2		3		3
Thomas Shepard	4	1	4	1	10		10

J. E. Jones	2	1	1		4	7	11
D. V. Norton	2	1		1	4		4
Bill J. Tomkins		1			1		1
John Henley		1			1		1
Lewis Grimsley		1		1	2		2
T. E. McCrackin	2	1		1	4	21	25
John Brynam	3	1	5	1	10		10
J. W. More	1	2	1		4	2	6
Ransom Sperlock		1	1	1	3		3
Lewis Johnson		1	1		2		2
William Hering	3	1	2	1	7	4	11
Stephen Grant	2	1		2	5		5
William Grant	2	1		1	4		4
Lewis Smith	4	1	2	1	8	2	10
John Sperlock		1	1		2		2
James Kent		1	1		2		2
Thomas Grice		1	1	1	3		3
George Condrie		1	1	1	3		3
Evander Lee		1			1		1
Arther Lee	2	1	2	3	8		8
John Smiley	5	1	5	2	13		13
Stephen Vann		1			1		1
Leonard Vann	1	1	1	1	4		4
H. W. Lewis	4	1	2	1	8	12	20
Daniel McClain		1			1	17	18

Thomas Hulin		1	1	1	3			3
Richard Head		1		1	2	6	3	11
Thomas Venter	1	1	1		3			3
Daniel Sinclair		1			1			1
J. H. Shepard	1	1	2	1	5			5
Lewis Hering		1		1	2			2
Robt. Dill	1	1	3	1	6	8		14
W. K. Holingsworth		1	2		3	2		5
W. J. Champion	2	2		2	6	3		9
H. J. Jenkins		1		1	2	5		7
Richard Head, Jr.	5	1	5	1	12			12
John Beasley	4	1	5	1	11			11
Samuel Wadkins	2	1	1	1	5			5
Ellis Dowlin	1	2		5	8	1		9
Nicholes Johnson	1	1		1	3			3
Jacob Williams		1			1			1
J. B. Baxley	3	1	2	1	7			7
Harmon Adams	1	1	1	1	4	1		5
Willey Oliver	4	1	1	2	8	7		15
John Vanright		1			1			1
John Oliver		1			1			1
Merkel Gills	4	1	3	1	9			9
William Flin		1			1			1
Samuel Feagens	7	1	3	1	12	14		26
Thomas Colmon	3	2	2	1	8			8
Daniel Steward	1	2			3			3

A. J. Colmon		1			1		1
W. J. Colmon		1			1		1
William Colmon	4	1	2	1	8	14	22
Micager Stinson	3	1	2	1	7	16	23
Duncan Malon	2	1	2	1	6	1	7
S. L. Byram	1	1		1	3		3
J. B. Stinson	2	1	3	2	8		8
Isaac Rodgers		1		2	3	1	4
Petter Rodgers	3	1	5	1	10		10
Daniel Caloway	1	1	6	1	9		9
N. C. Smith	4	1	2	1	8		8
J. C. Smith		1	2		3		3
Arthur Striplin	8	1	1	2	12	10	22
Aaron Striplin	4	1	3	1	9	6	15
Lochlin Camorn	3	1	2	1	7	3	10
Daniel McMelon	4	1	1	1	7	12	19
S. B. Picket	5	1	3	1	10	3	13
J. A. Saulsburg		1		1	2	6	8
W. S. Tailor	4	1	2	2	9	6	15
Margaret McIntosh	2		4	1	7	3	10
James Gorman	1	1		1	3	6	9
Jackson Morgan		1			1		1
E. Poston		1			1		1
Wilkins Bass		1	1		2		2
Georg McEarr (?)	1	1	1	2	5		5
Ben Stikes		1			1		1

W. Kingland		1			1			1
Wm. Pickard	2	1	2	1	6			6
W. J. Walley	4	2	2	1	9		1	10
J. M. Morrison	1	2		9	12	15		27
W. J. Ridgeal		1			1			1
J. Buckhanon		1			1			1
W. A. McKenzy	2	1	1	1	5	2		7
John Malon	2	1	1	1	5	3		8
J. F. Denis		1			1			1
Samuel Slate		1	1	1	3			3
Robt. Martain	5	1	2	1	9	13		22
J. I. Huddle		1	1	1	3			3
Edwin Mims	2	1	2	1	6			6
B. W. Weeks	3	1	3	1	8			8
Marke Sneargroves	1	1	6	1	9			9
John Mitchel	1	1	1		3			3
W. Fleming		1			1			1
E. Kirkpatrick	2	1	3	1	7	8		15
W. R. Hill		1			1			1
D. Steward		1			1			1
John Croley		1			1			1
S. S. Wakley		1			1			1
William Cowart	1	1		1	3	29		31
S. LeJar (?)	3	1	1	5	10	10		20
W. M. Bates		1		1	2	3		5
D. McNabe		1			1			1

G. W. Bates		1	3	1	5	2	7
John McKnab	1	1		1	3	2	5
Thomas Cargel	2	1	2	2	7	4	11
J. D. Bloodworth		1		1	2		2
E. C. Holemon		1			1	1	2
A. Holemon		1			1		1
A. McDonald		1		1	2	15	17
John McKasskill	1	1	1		3		3
Newson Hicks	3	1		1	5		5
Jeremiah Arington	1	1	2	1	5		5
Michael Hendricks		1		1	2	3	5
W. M. Tryon		1			1		1
Abraham Hamon		1			1		1
Joseph Morton	4	3		1	8	4	12
Lewis Odum	6	1		1	8		8
W. B. Mann	5	1	3	1	10	3	13
A. K. Hendricks	3	1		1	5	1	6
Samuel Brown	4			1	5	8	13
Aaron Smith	6	1	1	1	9		9
G. W. Winslit	1	1	5	1	8		8
H. W. Wiker		1			1		1
Daniel Nolain	2	1	1	1	5		5
Stephen Gibbens	1	1	1	1	4		4
Richard Sikes		1	1	1	3		3
William Beauchamp	6	3		1	10	15	25
W. N. Adkinson	2	1	4	1	8	2	10

Jeremiah Bass		1			1		1
William McRae	5	2	1	1	9		9
Wm. Arington	2	2	3	1	8		8
John Powers	1	1	1	1	4		4
Wm. Wilkins	6	1		1	8		8
Elisha Arington	2	1	2	1	6		6
John Gavis		2	1	1	4		4
Elisha Davis	2	1		1	4		4
John Sperlock		1		1	2		2
Robt. Hays	2	1	1	1	5		5
Joel Willis	3	2	3	1	9		9
Roderick Swain	1	1	1	1	4		4
Demsey Nowel		1	1	1	3		3
John Cook	2	2	2	2	8		8
Samuel Hearin	4	1	4	1	10		10
Joseph Daniel	2	2	4		8	4	12
Joel Dubose	5	2	3	1	11	2	13
Jarad Williams	5	2	4	1	12	2	14
Josiah Cole	2	1	4	1	8		8
Solomon Wood	2				2		2
Jesse Earley	1	1		1	3		3
Raborn Colins	4	1		1	6		6
John McKinis		1		1	2	5	7
John Cattinhead	2	1		1	4	2	6
F. R. Brown		1	4	1	6		6

Stephen Brown	1	1	1		3		3
Neacy Lewis		1	2		3	1	4
Adison Sapp	2	1			3	21	24
Joshua Lester	4	1	2		7	1	8
Jacob Odum		1		1	2	2	4
Levi Glass	2	1	6	1	10		10
A. S. Faulk	1	1	1		3		3
James Faulk	1	2	2	1	6		6
James Henderson		1			1		1
Lauchlin Curie		1	1	1	3	6	9
John McDonald		1			1		1
J. R. Tully	2	5	2	3	12	17	29
Jesse Lock		1	1		2		2
John Hering	1	1	3		5	6	11
Joshua Butts (?)		1	2		3	2	5
John Ray		1			1		1
Hardy Stricklin		1			1		1
Alexander Camell	4	5	1	3	14		14
L. J. Rouse	7	1	4	1	13	11	24
Barney Ruse		1	1	1	3		3
Willis Word		1		1	2		2
John Williamson	1	2	3	1	7		7
J. H. Graham	1	1	1	1	4		4
J. R. A. Williams		1	4	1	6		6
Michael Mathews	1	1		1	3		3
D. S. Arnold	1	1			2	4	6

William Cox	4	2	4	1	11		11
N. W. Turner	1	1	1	1	4		4
Burel Price	2	1	3	1	7		7
John Brewer		1			1		1
J. M. Lewis	5	1	3	1	10		10
Arden Keal		1	1	1	3		3
N. Walcutt		1			1		1
Jesse Birch	4	1	5	1	11	7	18
John Curie		1			1	16	17
Elisha Croley		1			1		1
W. R. Cowin		1			1		1
E. Young	2	1		1	4	1	5
James Young	1	1			2		2
Wm. McMaham	1	2	1	1	5	17	22
Tompson McMaham	1	2	1		4	1	5
Henry Saulsbury		1			1	1	2
J. M. McRae		1			1	1	2
W. B. Davis		1			1		1
John Stone		1			1		1
T. J. C. Hanson		1			1		1
Eh. Eason		1			1		1
G. W. Andrews	1	1		1	3		3
J. W. Powel		1	1	2	4	3	7
John Asque		1			1		1
J. H. Danforth		1			1		1
Clinton Pearson		2			2	21	23

Thomas Hogue		1			1		1
A. B. Holmon		1			1		1
Jacob Smith	2	2	1	1	6	3	9
R. C. Shorter	6	1	5	2	14	22	36
J. S. Swiney	1	1	1		3		3
J. J. Doser		1	1	1	3		3
G. W. Brantley		1	2	1	4		4
W. B. More		1			1		1
G. Coper	5	1	1	1	8	2	10
J. C. Browden		1			1	19	20
W. C. Fisher		1			1	4	5
John Quattlebum		1			1	3	4
William Simpson		1		1	2		2
Hiriam Carter	2	5		2	9		9
Partrick Willis	2	1	3	2	8		8
Thomas Row	2	2	1		5		5
J. R. Row	2	1	1	1	5		5
E. Hughbanks	2	1	2	1	6	2	8
Wesley Vinson	2	1	2	1	6	2	8
Marke Elmore	1	1		1	3		3
Daniel Morison	1	1	5	1	8	5	13
C. J. S. Kelly		1			1		1
A. Mason		1		1	2		2
A. A. McGowin	2	1	1	1	5		5
John Johnson	2	1	4		7		7
Thomas Flernoi	1	1	1	1	4	31	35

Josiah Flernois	1		2		3	30	33
Thomas Flernois		1		1	2	35	37
James Hering		1			1		1
W. P. Hering		1			1		1
Joseph Saulsbury	2	2		1	5	2	7
A. Stinson	3	2		1	6	7	13
Milton Browden		1			1	11	12
Richard Jacobs		2		2	4		4
William Archer	1	1	2	1	5		5
B. B. Barkdal		1		1	2	8	10
Isaac Fort		2			2	50	52
J. H. Hybert		1			1		1
A. B. Dail		2		1	3	2	5
William McCloud		1			1		1
William Worton	1	1		1	3		3
A. Treadwell	3	1	1	1	6	10	16
Samuel Marshal	2	1	1		4		4
William Hudson		1			1		1
John Welborn		1			1		1
S. M. Bowtain		2		1	3	4	7
James Hancock		1			1		1
Charles Hardewick		1			1		1
John McMelon	4	1	3		8	3	11
John S. F. Johns		1			1		1
John Brazel		1			1		1

H. Smith		1			1		1
William Miligan		1			1		1
C. W. Alexandria	3	1	1	1	6	3	9
E. J. Dickson	2	1	1	2	6		6
Cary Currie	3	1	3	1	8		8
B. Hopkins		1			1		1
Thomas Fail		1			1		1
T. H. Wood		1			1		1
R. A. Dunn		1			1		1
Joshua Baxley		1		1	2		2
Charles Eldridge		1			1		1
Dugal Blew		1			1		1
S. J. Slaughter		1			1		1
Henry McClendon		1	1		2		2
John Jones		1			1		1
F. S. Summercamp		1	1	1	3		3
H. Cole		1			1		1
S. Sanford		1			1		1
B. Watson	1	1	2		4	7	11
W. Pugh		1			1		1
S. E. Glen		1			1		1
Thomas Berry		1			1		1
S. Tober		1			1		1
A. Nash	1	2	1	3	7	4	11
T. Norfleet		1			1		1
Daniel McCloud	1	2	2	1	6		10

H. S. Samuels		1			1		1
Crofford Grizzel	2	1	1	1	5		5
A. Ross		1			1		1
N. Crofford		1			1		1
Andrew McKenzy		1			1		1
A. M. F. Mosley	2	1	1	1	5	1	6
John Parrimore	5	1	4	1	11		11
Moses Holon	2	1	2	1	6	3	9
B. Steward	2		1	1	4		4
Lewis Johnson	1	1	1	1	4		4
Willson Deshazo	3	1	1	1	6		6
George Lattimore		1			1		1
T. Barnet		1			1		1
Jesse Johns		1			1		1
M. Mason	4	1	2	1	8		8
John Monck		1			1		1
C. F. Gerkey		1		1	2		2
Hansford Dikes		1			1		1
Skelton Dennis	1	1	1	1	4		4
John Clarke	2	1	2	1	6		6
J. W. Elis	4	1	4	2	11		11
Joseph Thigpen	3	1	4	1	9		9
R. D. Landrum	2	1		1	4		4
Charnick Tharp		1	2	1	4		4
James Atwell	3	1	3	1	8		8
S. Bowen		1			1		1

James Richards		1	1	1	3	1	4
J. S. Williams	1	1	2	1	5	1	6
Arther Crews	3	2	3	1	9	15	24
James Dail	1	1	1	1	4		4
Lewis Mellon	3	1	4	1	9		9
James Swails	1	1	6	1	9	1	10
John W. Dennis		1			1		1
Andrew Gordon	2	1	2	1	6		6
L. S. More		1			1		1
T. W. Smith	2	1	1	1	5		5
Elis Frost	4	1	1	1	7		7
James Thomas		1			1		1
Robt. Smith		1			1		1
N. Stone		1			1		1
Jesse Harper		1	2	1	4		4
A. McCalister	2	1	2	1	6		6
L. Armstrong	2	1	2	1	6		6
R. W. McIntosh		1			1		1
D. McCardel		1			1		1
Wm. West		1			1		1
Samuel Michael		1			1		1
Cooly Mann		1			1		1
Samuel Thomas	5	1	2	1	9	2	11
John Cassetebill		1			1		1
John McCay		1			1		1

A. P. Crofford	1	1	1	1	4			4
Samuel Landrum		1			1			1
S. J. Parish	3	1	1	1	6	1		7
Thomas Roberson		1			1			1
H. H. Feald		1			1	5		6
W. S. Cowin	2	1		1	4	9		13
L. J. Laird	1	1	2		4	1	1	6
M. S. Elum	1	1	1		3			3
Jack Hardman		1	1	1	3	1		4
Antony McKinis		1			1			1
R. W. Nash		1			1			1
M. B. Nash		1			1			1
David McPhail	1	1	1		3	2		5
Z. J. Daniel	1	1	1	1	4	3		7
John W. Mann		1	4	1	6	6		12
Crofford Sprawl	2	3	3	1	9	7		16
Edward Williams	2	1	3	1	7	2		9
John P. Booth	2	1	2		5	28	1	34
Archibald Seals	4	1	2	1	8	11		19
John M. Lewis		1	1		2	5		7
Henry Saulsbury		1			1			1
Elias Morgan		1			1			1
John Searl		1			1			1
John Jarett		1			1			1
Isaac Nathanes	1	1	1	1	4	2		10

Henry Benton		1			1		1
Andrew Bulard	2	1	1	2	6		6
William Hays	2	1		1	4		4
Robt. Deshazo, Sr.	3	1	5	1	10		10
John Perkins		1		1	2	1	3
Ben Riley	2	1		1	4		4
Seaborn Hays	2	1	2	1	6		6
Aaron Kirkland		1	1	1	3		3
E. J. Ragan		1			1	10	11
D. F. Turner	4	1	4	1	10	1	11
Jimsey Cox	2	1	2	1	6		6
Abel Holder	2	1	1	1	5		5
Elias Lewis		1		2	3		3
David Holder		1			1		1
Hosse H. Williams	6	1	5		12		12
A. J. Simes	6	1	3	1	11		11
Charles Terrington		1		1	2	1	3
S. N. Brown	3	1	2	2	8	9	17
Luke Devilin		1			1		1
B. C. Williams		3	2	2	7	9	16
Malcomb Frasier	1	1		1	3		3
J. F. Denis		1			1		1
Reuben Willson	2	1	1	1	5		5
Churchwell Gormon		1	1	1	3	6	9
William Gormon	1		1	1	3	6	9
Richard Carroll		1			1		1

A. D. Void		1			1			1
Noah Stafford	1	1		2	4	2		6
Dugul McClain		1	1		2		1	3
L. Wharton	2	1	2	1	6	4		10
Frances Mulford			1	1	2			2
W. D. M. Freeman		1			1			1
B. R. Market		1			1			1
Philip Sage		1			1			1
Lemel Jones		1			1			1
Isaac Market		1			1			1
F. J. Blakey	2	1	2	1	6			6
Ed. James	3	1	4	1	9	2		11
Wm. Welborn	2	1	2	1	6	41	1	48
Asburn Reeves	2	1	5	1	9	4		13
A. Kilingsworth		1		1	2			2
George Gleson		1		1	2	1		3
Henry Blanket	1	1		1	3			3
Richard Smith		1	2	1	4			4
Wm. Danford		1			1			1
Joshua Hudson		1	2	1	4			4
Alfred Rouse		1			1	1		2
James Carr	3	1	1	1	6			6
A. Swaringam		1			1			1
Frederick Eikel		1			1			1
W. A. Pettit		1	1	2	4	3		7

James Ivins	2	1	4	1	8		8
John Gilmore	4	1		1	6		6
William King	1	1	1	2	5	1	6
Antony Windum	1	1		1	3		3
Wm. Bushop	1				1	9	10
John Martain	3	1	3	1	8	3	11
Robt. Bradley	4	1		1	6		6
Wm. Thompson	6	1	6	1	14		14
Jesse Sutton	1	1	7	1	10	1	11
Thomas Peoples	5	1	2	1	9		9
Robt. Teal	2	1	2	1	6		6
Philip Johnson, Sr.		1		1	2		2
John H. Dent		1	1	1	3	51	54
Abnor P nton	3	1	3	1	8	3	11
John Simons		1			1		1
David Simons		1			1		1
James Simons	2	1	2	1	6		6
William Anglin	3	1	4	1	9	1	10
Jacob Neace	1	1	2		4		4
Sarah Cole			1	1	2		2
John Powers	1	1	1	1	4		4
L. J. Keener	1	1	4	1	7	12	19
S. A. Simons	1	1	1	1	4		4
Arch Cook	5	1	4	4	14		14
Mathew Grimsley	3	1	2	1	7	5	12
Johnathan Williams	4	1	2	1	8		8

Alexandria Hardy	2	2	4	1	9		9
Adam Hardy	4	1		1	6		6
Eben George	3	4	3	1	11	3	14
J. W. Helums		1	1		2		2
Alen Tew		1			1		1
Charles Butts		1	1	1	3		3
Wiley Hardsog	3	1	1	2	7		7
Charles Helums	4	1		2	7		7
Bradford Long		1	1	1	3		3
Jesse Stricklen	2	2	8	2	14		14
Johnathan Tew	3	1		1	5		5
Jesse Hamm	2	3	1	3	9		9
Wm. Stephens	1	1	1	1	4		4
Joel Thomas	3	1	2	1	7		7
Thomas Hugus		1			1		1
Reuben Willson	2	1	1	1	5		5
John Helums	2	1	1	1	5		5
Petter Tew		1		1	2		2
William Dido		1	1		2		2
Nichols Zon	1	1	3	1	6	1	7
James Condrie	1	1	1	1	4		4
Thomas Shepard	2	1	4	2	9		9
John Mathews		1		1	2		2
Emanuel Thomas		1			1		1
Demsey Butts	1	1	2	1	5		5

H. Ooton (?) Octon		1			1		1
David Hardsog	3	1	7	1	12		12
Walter Tew	3	1		1	5		5
Henry Stricklin		1			1		1
T. C. Simons		1			1		1
William Young	3	1	2	1	7		7
John Helums	1	1	2	1	5		5
J. W. Pitman		1	3	1	5		5
David Dikes		1			1		1
Charlott Young	1			1	2		2
J. C. Benton		1	4	1	6	5	11
T. J. Winfield		1	1		2		2
David Hamm		1			1		1
J. Lovett	5	1	4	1	11	1	12
John Benton	3	1	4	1	9		9
Rusel Bones	1	1	1	1	4		4
Austain Nichols		1	3	1	5		5
John Willis	1	1		1	3		3
R. C. Roberson		1		1	2		2
Malcom McClain		1			1		1
John Chaney	1	1		1	3		3
S. Mathews	2	1	1		4		4
Lewis Walker		1	1	1	5		5
Willis Carole	1	2	7	1	11		11
Isaac Benton	2		2	1	5		5

B. Lampley		1	1		2		2
Jacob Little		1	2	1	4		4
George Landrum	1	1	1	2	5	1	6
A. T. Wells		1			1		1
James Cason		1		1	2		2
B. Landrum		1			1		1
John Ivins		1	4	2	7		7
Michael Stone	5	2		1	8		8
Lovet McClain	2	1	1	1	5		5
Eliga Monias	5	1		1	7		7
Elgit Drisktol		1	3		4		4
George Cabbiness	4	1	1		6	1	7
R. C. Ethridge	2	1		1	4	1	5
Micaja Alen	1	1	2	1	5		5
J. M. Cabbiness		1	2	1	4		4
John Smith		1	2	1	4		4
William Thomas	7	1	7	1	16		16
John C. Smith	3	2	3	2	10	1	11
Mathew Bery	1	1		1	3		3
Pardon Bulock	1	1	4	1	7		7
Henry Wells	1	1	2	1	5	1	6
Berry Wells	2	1	1	1	5		5
T. C. Clark	1	1	1	1	4		4
Clinton Wood	1	1	1	1	4		4
Wm. Fouch	1	1		1	3		3

Waren Norris	1	1	1	1	4		4
Elizabeth Tharp			2	1	3		3
James Baker, Sr.		1		2	3	3	6
James Baker, Jr.	2	1	3	1	7		7
Robt. Baker	3	1	3	1	8		8
Richard Bush		1	1	1	3		3
Rial Jones	4	1	4	1	10		10
Zekel Wise	7	1	3	1	12		12
Wm. Jones		1			1		1
Thomas Linsey	3	1	1	1	6		6
Morton Melon	6	1	2	1	10		10
Samuel Breland	3	1	4	1	9		9
Solomon Creal	3	1	2	1	7		7
Stephen Lee	5	2	3	1	11		11
Elizabeth Lee	2		2	2	6		6
J. Valentine		1		1	2		2
Jeremiah Tetston (?)		1			1		1
Joseph Cradock	1	1			2	1	3
Timothy Lee	3	1	1	2	7		7
Henry Perswell		1		1	2		2
John McClendon	2	1	1	1	5		5
Gabril Perswell	3	1	3	1	8		8
J. A. Williams	4	1	3	1	9		9
Asa Dubose	1	1	2	1	5		5
James Lee	2	1		1	4	1	5

Andrew Lee		1	1	1	3		3
Martain Miller	2	1	2	1	6		6
Moses Harvel	1	1	2	1	5		5
Jesse Browning	7	1	3	1	12		12
Jackson Browning		1	1		2		2
Robt. Richards	1	1		1	3	5	8
Wm. Richards	1	1	4	1	7	4	11
Thomas Richards	5	1	1	1	8		8
Normon Weatherby	1	1	1		3		3
Arthur Crofford	1	2	2	1	6		6
Fearn Wood		1	1		2		2
William Holmes	2	1	4	1	8		8
Young Wood	3	2	1	1	7		7
John Searsey	2	2	2	1	7		7
Bryant Berham	1	1	1	1	4		4
Blake Balard	1	1		1	3		3
Edward Berham	2	2	2	1	7		7
James Wood	1	2	3	1	7		7
John Mitchel	1	1	1		3		3
H. L. Pinkerton		1	1	1	3		3
David Pinkerton		1		1	2		2
Stephen Batman		1			1		1
John Thernin (?)		1	2	1	4		4
Daniel Fergerson		1			1		1
W. D. Jerdain	2	1	2	1	6		6

F. W. Boyd		1	1		2		2
W. A. Broadaway	2	1	2	1	6		6
J. Broadaway		1	1		2		2
James McCleanon	1	1	1	1	4		4
J. W. Scott		1	1	1	3		3
Henry Hill	2	1	2	1	6	6	12
John McClendon	4	1	3	1	9	4	13
William Avret	3	2	2	1	8	2	10
William Cliatt		1	1		2	18	20
Owen Ivy	2	1	3	1	7		7
Moses Parker	3	1		1	5		5
John Hays	1	1	2	1	5		5
James Cannon		1			1		1
A. Glen		1			1		1
J. E. Glenn	4	2	2		8	8	16
Henry Tolston	1	1	2	1	5		5
John Smith	1	1	2	1	5		5
David Dane		1		1	2		2
John Willis		1			1		1
Caleb Cox	6	1	1	1	9		9
Wm. Tharp	1	1	1		3		3
J. M. More	1	1	2		4	2	6
Lucy More			1	1	2	2	4
W. J. Clark	2	1	4	1	8		8
W. J. W. Wilborn		1		1	2		2

Name							Total
A. B. Dail		1			1		1
Andrew Spears	1	1	1	1	4	2	6
Aaron Parker		1		1	2	1	3
William Lipscomb		1	1	1	3		3
George Preacher	4	8	1	2	15	20	35
Culin Battel	2	1	1	1	5	122	127
W. D. Grimes		1		1	2	50	52
C. C. Mills	5	1	5	1	12	30	42
A. McCalister	2	1	2	1	6		6
A. McPearson	1	1	4	1	7		7
William Williams		1			1		1
W. R. Hays		1		1	2		2
Samuel Row	2	2	1		5		5
Thomas Row	2	1	1	1	5		5
John R. Row	2	1	2	1	6		6
James Stokes		1			1		1
Jacob Stephens	4	1	3	1	9		9
A. Stinson	3	2		1	6		6
Miles Barfield	2	1		1	4		4
Timothy Hudson	1	1	1	1	4		4
B. A. Alexandria	3	1	3	1	8	12	20
James Whittemore		2	1	1	4		4
John Moody		1			1		1
D. Newman		1			1		1
J. N. Harper		1		2	3		3
L. Brown	2	1	4	1	8		8

Thomas Bevil	3	1	4	1	9		9
C. A. Winters		1			1		1
Owen Mury		1			1		1
Eliza Hays	1	1	1	1	4		4
Silas Baily		1	1	1	3		3
Mathew Cabbiness		2			2		2
James Muckilvill		7			7		7
Seth Pitman		1	3	1	5		5
Robt. Brooks		1		1	2		2
A. Brainard		1		1	2		2
Archibald Barfield		1		1	2		2
Samuel Wiseman		1	1	1	3		3
Hansel Keal	2	1	2	1	6	1	7
Jacob Woodcock	1	1	2	1	5		5
Wheat Pynes	2	1		1	4		4
William Tate	3	1	2		6		6
S. E. Hart		1			1		1
J. S. Linsey	1	1	3	1	6		6
David Wattson	1	1	1	1	4		4
Sarah Benton	3		2	1	6		6
William Hartley		1	2	1	4		4
Martain Tiller		1			1		1
Willey Stricklin	5	1	6	1	13		13
W. K. Faulk		1	1	1	3	2	5
Nathan Minsey	1	1	2	1	5		5
E. Andrews		1			1		1

John Brown	3	1	3	1	8		8
Bertis Bird	1	1	1	1	4		4
James Chambers		1	2		3		3
John Car	1	1	1	1	4		4
Johnathan Harison	5	1	3	1	10		10
William Black	3	1	2	1	7		7
Hosey Edins	1	1	1	1	4		4
John Barclay	3	1	1	1	6		6
Abslam Mooney		1			1		1
Malcom McNair		1			1		1
Thomas Downer	2	2	2	1	7		7
John Garner		1	3	1	5		5
Benet Bizzel	1	1	2	1	5	13	18
Bryant Farrior	3	1	3	2	9	2	11
Robt. Tilman	4	1	4	1	10		10
Alfred West	2	1	2	1	6		6
Daniel McDonald	2	1	6	1	10		10
Miles McInis	1	1	1		3		3
David Aplin	1	1	2	1	5		5
Henry Faulk	3	1	3	1	8	10	18
Everette Loveless		1		1	2		2
Jacob Minsey		1	2	1	4	4	8
John Hoskins		1			1		1
R. Bird	2	1	3	1	7		7
Thomas L. Grant	1	1	2	1	5		5
David Powel	2	1	4	1	8		8

James Strength	2	1	3	1	7	1	8
John Harison		1	1		2		2
Rusel Campbell	1	1	1	1	4		4
A. Campbell		1			1		1
W. Cox		1			1		1
Wm. Campbell		1			1		1
C. C. Johnes		1		1	2		2
Robt. Bankes	2	1	1	1	5	1	6
Daniel Campbell		1	2	1	4		4
W. A. Cox	4	2	3	2	11		11
H. N. Bizzell	2	1	1	1	5	1	6
James Casey	3	1	2	1	7		7
John Dansby	3	1	2	1	7	2	9
John Ivins		1			1		1
Joseph Ivins		1			1		1
Samuel Sasser		1			1		1
John Sasser	2	1	1	1	5		5
Samuel Everette	1	1	1		3		3
Ransom Campbell	1	1		1	3		3
John Minsey	3	1	3	1	8		8
Jacob Minsey, Sr.		1		1	2		2
George Nichols	3	1	1	1	6		6
James Barclay		1			1		1
Rachael Dove (?)			2	1	3		3
William Hutcheson	5	1	3	1	10		10
John Campbell		1	2	1	4		4

James Grimsley	1	1	1		3		3
Charles Williamson	5	1	3	1	10		10
George Parmer	1	2	4	1	8		8
Thomas Higre (?)		1			1		1
Henry M. Hum---		1		1	2		2
Warrie Killpartrick	6	1	2	2	11		11
A. T. Spence	1	1	2	1	5		5
William Head	7	1	3	1	12	4	16
John Bass	2	1	5	1	9		9
J. L. Hunter	2	3	5	2	12	120	132
Abreham Danford	8	2	1	1	12		12
William Boyd		1		1	2	6	8
Jeremiah Kingstond		1			1		1
John Hardy		1			1		1
J. R. Wilkins	1	1	1	1	4		4
James Trawick	1	1	2	1	5	9	14
W. M. McMurry	3	1		2	6		6
B. Vinson	1	2	1	2	6		6
Lorenzo Faulk		1	2	1	4	1	5
Judy Medley	1	2		2	5		5
Hansel Medley		1			1		1
Eldridge Medley	1	1	1	1	4		4
Early Kilpartrick	2	1		1	4		4
James Langley	3	1	4	1	9		9
James McRory	3	1	2	1	7		7
John Condrie	2	1	3	1	7		7

Stephen Griggars	1	1	1	1	4		4
Archibald Ray	2	2	1	2	7		7
Jesse Lewis		1			1		1
Jesse Jones		1			1		1
W. K. Jones	4	1	2	1	8		8
George Jerry	3	1	2	1	7		7
J. T. Railey		1			1		1
John Nawls	4	1	4	1	10		10
Gary King	3	1	2	1	7		7
John Smith		1	2	1	4		4
Joshua Tailor	1	1	2	1	5		5
Charles Williamson	5	1	3	1	10		10
Seaborn Jones	2	1	4	1	8	7	15
Gilbert Mann		1			1	2	3
Hobes Bradley	1	1			2	1	3
James Brantley		1	1	1	3		3
William Sperlock	3	1	1	1	6		6
Henry Jones	1	1	1	1	4		4
F. F. Wood		1	1		2		2
B. C. Beard	4	3	4	2	13	11	24
William Green	7	1			8		8
Jeptha Linsey	2	1	1	1	5		5
John Bulard	1	1	3	1	6	2	8
Willey Stricklen	5	2	6	1	14		14
Mgw. Davenport	2	1	4	1	8		8
Joseph Ramsay		1	4	2	7		7

Egw. Hays		1			1			1
William Abney	1	1	2	1	5	85		90
Joseph Owens	4	1	4	1	10			10
Isaac Willkins	1		1		2			2
F. W. Pugh	2	1	2	1	6	8		14
Egw. Clark		1	1	1	3			3
Nathaniel Reader		1	2	1	8			8 *
Moses Thomas	3	1	3	1	8			8
William Night	4	1		1	6			6
Alex. Gillis	3	2	1	1	7			7
John Chane	4	2	5	2	13	18		31
James Martin		1	1	1	3	2		5
James Bulard		1	2	1	4	1		5
James W. Seals	2	1	1	1	5	1	1	7
A. W. Jones		1			1			1
William Flack	1	2	3	1	7	15		22
Henry Jerry	1	1		1	3			3
James Tucker	3	1	3	1	8	5		13
Willey Williams	1		2	1	4			4
Samuel Southwait	2	1	2		5			5
T. C. McDowel	2	1	7	1	11	2		13
William Bears	2	2	4	1	9			9
James Steward	1	1	4	1	7	2		9
Liven Faulk	1	1	1	1	4			4
Abraham Johnson		1		1	2			2

Note: Copied as recorded. Correct total should be 4.

George Sisemore	1	2		1	4		4
Duncan Culbrith		1	1	1	3		3
G. W. Trainum	4	1	3	1	9		9
Rolin Pulin	4	1	3	1	9		9
J. M. Raines		1			1	15	16
William Thomas	7	1	7	2	17		17
G. L. Johnson	6	1	4	3	14		14
W. Hall		1			1		1
Luke Elmore	3	1	3	1	8		8
John Green	4	1	4	1	10		10
John Smith	3	2			5		5
Edward Houstain	1	1	2	2	6		6
B. Alen	6	3		1	10		10
Willey Titwell	2	2	3	1	8		8
Willy Johns	4	1	2	2	9		9
John Clarke	1	1		1	3		3
N. J. Baker	2	1	2	1	6		6
Wm. Dobes		1			1		1
John McKasskill	2	1	2	1	6		6
E. McKasskill	1	1	1	1	4		4
D. McKasskill	2	1	2	1	6		6
R. McKasskill	4	1	2	1	8		8
B. Loveless	1	1	2	1	5		6
W. B. Files	5	1	3	2	11		11
Neal McNorton		1			1		1

Sion Hill		1			1		1
Zachariah Williams	2	3		4	9	97	106
Joseph Caloway	2	1	2	1	6		6
Zachariah Bush	5	1	4	1	11	10	21
B. Farmer	1	1		1	3		3
Martain Johnson		1	5	1	7		7
Martain Cleaveland		1			1		1
Hugh McDonald		1	1	1	3	23	26
Nathan Reader	3	1	3	2	9		9
Alexw. Clelly (?)	2	1	2	1	6		7
Isham Caswell	3	1	2	2	8	3	11
Lovand Lee	1	1	1	1	4	3	7
Thomas Harod		1	1	1	3		3
Bery Parmer	1	1	1	1	4		4
John McGilbery	3	1		1	5		5
Hampton Lisles	2	1	3	1	7		7
Parton Bulock	1	1	4	1	7		7
C. McClain	2	1	1	1	5		5
Irvin Hanley	2	1	1	1	5		5
W. McPhaden		1	2	1	4		4
L. A. T. Johnson		1	2		3	1	4
Doly Brown	3		3	1	7	5	12
Alexw. Gillis	3	2	1	2	8		8
John Emerson	5	1	1	1	8		8
James Tiler		1		1	2		2
Jacob Parmer	2	1	4	3	10	1	11

W. Gilmore	1	1	1	1	4		4
T. Kilingsworth	1	1	3	1	6		6
B. H. Emerson	1	1	2	1	5		5
J. J. Tramel	1	1	3	1	6	10	16
Shadk. Dikes		1		1	2		2
John Shipes	2	1	2	1	6		6
W. Merphrey	3	1	3	1	8		8
Isak Sanders		1	1		2		2
John Crabtree		1	5	3	9		9
D. McGilbery		1			1		1
A. Weatherby	3	1	2	2	8	18	26
John Cotton	2	1	3	1	7	6	13
A. R. Torrence		1			1	8	9
James Titwell	2	1	3	1	7	11	18
Jese Grizzel	2	1	2	1	6		6
James Avant	2	1	3	1	7	19	26
Thomas Tatum	1	1		1	3	11	14
Joseph Tatum	2	1	2	1	6	13	19
Daniel Groit	1	1	4	2	8		8
James Houstain	1	1	1	1	4	2	6
Thomas Mathews	1	1	2	1	5		5
W. Paulden	1	1	1	1	4	9	13
John Scott	3	1	1	1	6	1	7
James Grizzel	1	1	1		3		3
J. N. Jones	1	1	2	1	5		5
W. Parkehill	2	1	2	1	6		6

Name								Total
Thomas Kent	3	1	4	1	9			9
W. Gordon		1			1			1
J. Finch		1	1	1	3			3
William Griffin	1	1	2	1	5			5
G. L. Berry	1	1		1	3	4		7
Elizabeth Baily	4		3	1	8	7		15
A. Shanks	3	1	3	1	8			8
James Shanks	2	1	4	1	8			8
Lucy Euford	1			1	2	21		23
Elizabeth Warren		1		2	3	13		16
Daniel Ivins		1		1	2			2
Sarah Lewis				1	1	7		8
John Barfield		1		1	2			2
John Deshazo	2	1	3	1	7			7
H. M. Tomkins	1	1	2	2	6	11		17
Nancy Venters	2		1	1	4	6		10
W. Loveless	2	1	3	1	7	4		11
Jacob Lampley	7	1	2	1	11	8		19
L. Crosley	1		3	2	6	3		9
J. D. Seals		1	1		2			2
B. T. White	2	1	2	1	6	2		6 *
Total amount	1926	1480	1853	1021	6280	2980	23	9283

* Note: Copied as recorded. Correct total should be 8.

Abney, Wm., 50
Adam, Wm. B., 16
Adams, Baker, 11
Adams, Harmon, 22
Adkinson, W. N., 25
Adkinson, Wm., 6
Alen, B., 51
Alen, Micaja, 40
Alexander, B. A., 44
Alexander, C. W., 44
Alstin, John, 8
Alums, Wm., 14
Anderson, Henry, 5
Anderson, John H., 10
Andrews, E., 45
Andrews, G. W., 28
Anglin, Franklin, 18
Anglin, Wm., 37
Aplin, David, 46
Archer, Wm., 30
Arington, Elisha, 16, 26
Arington, Jeremiah, 25
Arington, Wm., 2, 26
Armstrong, J. B., 5
Armstrong, L., 33
Armstrong, W. J., 4
Arnold, D. S., 27
Asque, John, 28
Atwell, James, 32
Aullman, Jordan, 7
Avent, James, 53
Avret, Wm., 43
Ayrz, W. H., 2

Bailey, John, 2
Baily, Elizabeth, 54
Baily, Hosey, 13
Baily, Silas, 45
Baker, H. W., 1
Baker, James, Jr., 41
Baker, James, Sr., 41
Baker, Larkis, 8
Baker, N. J., 51
Baker, Robt., 41
Baker, Waren, 20
Balard, Blake, 42
Ball, Hartwell, 4
Balldee, P. H., 5
Bankes, Robt., 47
Barclay, James, 47
Barclay, John, 46
Barfield, Arch., 45
Barfield, Miles, 44
Barkdal, B. B., 30
Barnet, T., 32

Bass, Andrew, 6
Bass, Elias, 10
Bass, James, 3
Bass, Jeremish, 26
Bass, John, 48
Bass, Josiah, 4
Bass, Wilkins, 23
Bates, G. W., 25
Bates, W. M., 24
Batman, Stephen, 42
Battel, Culin, 44
Baxley, J. B., 22
Baxley, James, 10
Beard, B. C., 49
Bearfield, Grady, 1
Beard, B. C., 49
Bears, Wm., 50
Beasley, Charles, 12
Beasley, James, 11
Beasley, John, 22
Beasley, Wm., 10
Beauchamp, Green, 11
Beauchamp, Wm., 25
Bell, John, 18
Bell, Samuel, 8
Bell, Talbot, 3
Bell, Willis, 17
Benet, Ryan, 17
Bennet, Redmon, 3
Bennett, Seth, 2
Benson, G., 13
Benton, Henry, 35
Benton, Isaac, 39
Benton, J. C., 39
Benton, John, 39
Benton, Right, 19
Benton, Sarah, 45
Berham, Bryant, 42
Berham, Edward, 42
Berlemy (?), David, 16
Berlison, see Burleson
Berlison, A. D., 17
Berlison, Aaron, 1
Berry, G. L., 54
Berry, Thomas, 31
Bery, Mathew, 40
Bevil, Thomas, 45
Bigford, J., 11
Birch, Jesse, 28
Bird, Bertis, 46
Bird, Jesse, 28
Bird, R., 46
Bizzel, Benet, 46
Bizzel, Curtis, 7

Champion, W. J., 22
Chane, John, 50
Chaney, Ann, 1
Clark, Egw., 50
Clark, T. C., 40
Clark, W. J., 43
Clarke, James, 2
Clarke, John, 32, 51
Clelly, Alexw., 52
Clemons, James, 17
Cleveland, Martain, 52
Cliatt, Wm., 43
Cloyd, W., 2
Cole, D. J., 1
Cole, G. J., 1
Cole, H., 31
Cole, James, 8
Cole, John C., 3
Cole, Josiah, 26
Cole, Sarah, 37
Colins, Raborn, 26
Collins, Willson, 8
Colmon, A. J., 23
Colmon, Jesse B., 3
Colmon, Thomas, 22
Colmon, W. J., 23
Colmon, Wm., 23
Condrie, Denis, 10
Condrie, George, 21
Condrie, James, 38
Condrie, John, 48
Cook, Arch, 37
Cook, John, 26
Cooper, A. D., 16
Cooper, Wm., 4
Coper, G., 29
Cotton, John, 53
Cotton, Richard, 18
Cowart, Wm., 24
Cowin, W. R., 28
Cowin, W. S., 34
Cox, A. J., 6
Cox, Caleb, 43
Cox, Edward, 8
Cox, Emanuel, 8
Cox, Jemsey, 35
Cox, W., 47
Cox, W. A., 47
Crabtree, John, 53
Cradler, Cary, 9
Craddock, Joseph, 41
Creach, W. C., 12
Creal, Lewis, 9
Creal, Solomon, 41
Crews, Arther, 33

Crofford, A. P., 34
Crofford, Arthur, 42
Crofford, N., 32
Croley, Elisha, 28
Croley, John, 24
Crosley, L., 54
Culbrith, Duncan, 51
Cuningham, John, 7
Cuningham, Ucal, 13
Cunningham, Duncan, 14
Curie, John, 28
Curie, Lauchlin, 27
Currie, Angush, 9
Currie, Cary, 31
Currie, Daniel, 9
Currie, Hugh, 1
Currie, Michael, 17

Dail, A. B., 30, 44
Dail, James, 33
Dane, David, 43
Danford, Abraham, 48
Danford, Wm., 36
Danforth, J. H., 28
Daniel, Joseph, 26
Daniel, Robert, 1
Daniel, Seaborn, 12
Daniel, Z. J., 34
Dansby, Isham, 6
Dansby, John, 47
Davenport, Mgw., 49
Davis, G. S., 14
Davis, John, 14
Davis, W. B., 28
Davis, Wm., 17
Day, Emory, 19
Dennis, J. F., 24, 35
Denis, Skelton, 32
Dennis, John W., 33
Dent, John H., 37
Deshazo, J. E., 20
Deshazo, John, 54
Deshazo, Robert, 20
Deshazo, Robert, Sr., 35
Deshazo, Willson, 32
Devilin, Luke, 35
Dickson, E. J., 31
Dickson, Wm., 3
Dido, Wm., 38
Dikes, David, 39
Dikes, Hansford, 32
Dikes, Shadk., 53
Dill, Robert, 22
Dobes, Wm., 51
Dolton, Triston, 1

Dorman, Mason, 11
Dorman, Rinza, 7
Dorman, Wm., 4
Doser, J. J., 29
Dove (?), Rachael, 47
Dowlin, Ellis, 22
Downer, Thomas, 46
Doyle, H. J., 1
Drisktol, Elgit, 40
Dubose, Asa, 41
Dubose, Joel, 26
Duglass, John, 6
Dunn, J. M., 20
Dunn, R. A., 31

Earley, Jesse, 26
Eason, Eh., 28
Edge, J. W., 4
Edins, Hosey, 46
Edins, J. H., 9
Eidson, Edw., 15
Eidson, John, 17
Eidson, Rody, 10
Eikel, Frederick, 36
Eldridge, Charles, 31
Elis, J. W., 32
Elis, John, 16
Elmore, Alfred, 1
Elmore, Luke, 51
Elmore, Marke, 29
Elum, M. S., 34
Emerson, B. H., 53
Emerson, John, 52
Ethridge, R. C., 40
Euford, Lucy, 54
Euford, T. C., 5
Everette, Samuel, 47

Fail, Thomas, 31
Farior, Bryant, 8
Farmer, B., 52
Farrior, Bryant, 46
Farrior, David, 10
Farrior, John, 7
Faulk, A. S., 27
Faulk, A. W., 10
Faulk, H. L., 9
Faulk, Henry, 46
Faulk, Henry, Jr., 8
Faulk, J. S., 13
Faulk, James, 9, 17
Faulk, Levin, 50
Faulk, Lorenzo, 48
Faulk, Thomas, 14
Faulk, W. K., 45
Feagins, Samuel, 22

Feald, H. H., 34
Fealder, Isham, 20
Fearcloth, Rayford, 7
Fenn, Mathew, 16
Fergerson, Daniel, 42
Fergeson, Angish, 14
Files, W. B., 51
Filugan, Benj., 16
Filyeaw, W. G., 1
Finch, J., 54
Fisher, W. C., 29
Flack, Wm., 50
Fleming, W., 24
Flernoi, Josiah, 30
Flernoi, Thomas, 29, 30
Flin, Wm., 22
Floid, J., 19
Flowers, Abner, 10
Flowers, Willis, 10
Fort, Isaac, 30
Foster, Beauford, 8
Fouch, Wm., 40
Franklin, Benj., 13
Frasier, Malcomb, 35
Freeman, W. D. M., 36
Frost, Elis, 33
Fulgem, Rayfor, 16
Fulton, Duncan, 14

Gandy, Wm., 17
Gansy, W. H., 18
Garner, John, 10, 46
Garvis, George, 5
Gary, Richard, 1
George, Eben, 38
Gerkey, C. F., 32
Gibbens, Stephen, 25
Gibbins, Robert, 3
Gibson, W. C., 11
Giles, Daniel, 15
Gilman, George, 9
Gilmore, John, 37
Gilmore, W., 53
Gillmore, George, 13
Gillis, Alex., 50, 52
Gillis, Rynal, 3
Gills, Markel, 22
Glass, Levi, 27
Glass, Littleton, 10
Glass, W. J., 12
Glen, A., 43
Glen, J. E., 43
Glen, S. E., 31
Gleson, George, 36
Gooden, George, 5
Goodson, B. W., 1

Gordon, Andrew, 33
Gordon, W., 54
Gorman, James, 23
Gormon, Churchwell, 35
Gormon, John, 4
Gormon, Wm., 16, 35
Gought, W. H., 16
Grady, Henry, 5
Graham, J. H., 27
Graham, James, 13
Graham, John, 19
Graham, W. C., 13
Gramberry, J. B., 17
Grant, John, 18
Grant, Stephen, 21
Grant, Thomas L., 46
Grant, Wm., 21
Gray, (Guy?), Lewis, 6
Gray, Thomas, 2
Green, Henchy, 10
Green, John, 6, 51
Green, Wm., 49
Grice, Thomas, 21
Griffin, Wm., 54
Griggars, Stephen, 49
Griggs, Thomas, 4
Grimes, W. D., 44
Grimsley, James, 48
Grimsley, Lewis, 21
Grimsley, Mathew, 37
Griset, Daniel, 6
Grizzel, James, 53
Grizzel, Jese, 53
Groit, Daniel, 53
Grubs, Adam, 8
Grubs, Wm., 4
Gunter, Leroy, 15
Guy, Lewis, 6

Hall, Daniel, 14
Hall, Henry, 14
Hall, John, 20
Hall, Samuel, 18
Ham, Jesse, 4
Ham, Partrick, 3
Hamm, David, 39
Hamm, Jesse, 38
Hamon, Abraham, 25
Hancock, Elisha, 17
Hancock, James, 30
Hancock, W. S., 3
Hanley, Irvin, 52
Hanson, T. J., C., 28
Hardman, Jack, 34
Hardsog, David, 39

Hardsog, Wiley, 38
Hardwick, Chas., 30
Hardy, Adam, 38
Hardy, Alexr., 38
Hardy, John, 48
Hardy (?), W. H., 15
Harelson, Josiah, 3
Harelson, Moses, 9
Hargroves, Henry, 10
Harison, John, 46
Harison, Jonathan, 46
Harod, Thomas, 52
Harper, Abslom, 1
Harper, J. N., 44
Harper, Jesse, 33
Harrison, Wm., 14
Hart, S. E., 45
Hart, Stephen, 19
Hartley, Wm., 45
Harvel, Moses, 42
Hays, Egw., 50
Hays, Eliza, 45
Hays, John, 43
Hays, Robert, 26
Hays, Samuel, 7
Hays, Seaborn, 35
Hays, W. R., 44
Hays, Wm., 35
Head, Richard, 22
Head, Richard, Jr., 22
Head, Wm., 48
Hearin, Samuel, 26
Helms, Aaron, 5
Helms, Hardy, 9
Helms, Nathaniel, 8
Helum, Joel, 8
Helums, Abraham, 6
Helums, Charles, 38
Helums, J. W., 38
Helums, John, 36, 39
Henderson, James, 27
Hendricks, A. K., 25
Hendricks, Michael, 25
Henly, John, 21
Henry, Wm., 16
Hering, Arba, 7
Hering, Edward, 4
Hering, James, 30
Hering, John, 27
Hering, Lewis, 22
Hering, W. P., 30
Hering, Wm., 21
Herring, Grady, 10
Herring, Ichabod, 19
Herring, Ivy, 19

Herring, West, 18
Hicks, Newsom, 25
Highland, Petter, 8
Higre (?), Thomas, 48
Hill, Henry, 43
Hill, Sion, 52
Hill, W. R., 24
Hines, Wiley, 17
Hinson, Wm., 19
Hobdy, Robert, 17
Hobdy, Thomas, 10
Hogue, Thomas, 29
Holden, Jesse, 15
Holder, David, 35
Holeman, A., 25
Holeman, E. C., 25
Holin (?), John, 15
Holingsworth, W. K., 22
Holman, A. B., 29
Holman, Thomas, 20
Holman, Wm., 17
Holme, Alen, 3
Holmes, Wm., 42
Holon (?), Moses, 32
Hood, B. R., 4
Hood, Daniel, 3
Hood, J. P., 2
Hopkins, B., 31
Horn, Nathan, 12
Horton, G. W., 3
Hoskins, John, 46
Houstain, Edward, 51
Houstain, James, 53
Huddle, J. I., 24
Hudson, Joshua, 36
Hudson, Timothy, 44
Hudson, Wm., 30
Hughs, Daniel, 17
Hugus, Thomas, 38
Huland, Riley, 13
Hulin, Thomas, 22
Hum----, Henry M., 48
Hunter, J. L., 48
Hutcheson, Wm., 47
Hybert, J. M., 30

Ivins, Daniel, 54
Ivins, Isham, 3
Ivins, J. M., 15
Ivins, James, 37
Ivins, John, 40, 47
Ivins, Joseph, 47
Ivins, Turner, 19
Ivy, John, 6
Ivy, Owen, 43

Jackson, F. S., 15
Jackson, G. W., 3
Jackson, J. C., 16
Jackson, Jasmith, 10
Jackson, John, 2
Jackson, John R., 16
Jackson, John W., 9
Jacobs, Richard, 30
James, Ed., 36
Jarret, John, 34
Jenkins, H. J., 22
Jerdain, W. D., 42
Jernigan, David, 15
Jerry, George, 49
Jerry, Henry, 49
Johns, C. C., 47
Johns, Francis, 2
Johns, Jesse, 32
Johns, John S. F., 30
Johns, Wm., 15
Johns, Willy, 51
Johnson, Abraham, 50
Johnson, Alen, 10
Johnson, Alexr., 19
Johnson, G. L., 51
Johnson, J. E., 19
Johnson, Jesse, 16
Johnson, John, 29
Johnson, L. A. T., 32
Johnson, Lewis, 21, 32
Johnson, Martain, 52
Johnson, Nicholes, 22
Johnson, Phelex, 18
Johnson, Philip, 3
Johnson, Philip, Sr., 37
Johnson, Timothy, 2
Jones, A. W., 50
Jones, Henry, 49
Jones, J. E., 21
Jones, J. N., 53
Jones, Jesse, 49
Jones, John, 31
Jones, Lemuel, 36
Jones, Rial, 41
Jones, Seaborn, 49
Jones, W. K., 49
Jones, Wm., 41

Keal, Arden, 28
Keal, Hansel, 45
Keiner, G. B., 18
Keiner, L. J., 37
Keiner, T. B., 20
Kelly, Alexr., 4
Kelly, C. J. S., 29

Squires, Willey, 19
Stafford, Noah, 36
Stephens, Jacob, 44
Stephens, W. F., 19
Stephens, W. J., 4
Stephens, Wm., 38
Stephens, James, 7
Steward, Alexr., 13
Steward, B., 32
Steward, D., 24
Steward, D. S., 13
Steward, Daniel, 22
Steward, J. S., 14
Steward, James, 50
Steward, John, 14
Stikes, Ben., 23
Stinson, A., 30, 44
Stinson, George, 10
Stinson, J. B., 23
Stinson, Micager, 23
Stokes, Henry, 5
Stokes, James, 44
Stone, John, 28
Stone, N., 33
Stone, Michael, 40
Strength, James, 47
Stricklin, Hardy, 27
Stricklin, Henry, 39
Stricklin, Jesse, 38
Stricklin, J. W., 6
Stricklin, Willey, 45, 49
Striplin, Aaron, 23
Striplin, Arthur, 23
Stutz, Sharevick, 11
Summercamp, F. S., 31
Sutton, Charles, 13
Sutton, Jesse, 37
Swails, James, 33
Swaringam, A., 36
Swiney, J. S., 29

Tailor, John, 1
Tailor, Joshua, 49
Tailor, Kinson, 7
Tailor, W. S., 23
Tanzy, David, 6
Tate, Wm., 45
Tatum, Joseph, 53
Tatum, Thomas, 53
Teal, Robert, 37
Teat, Isaac, 9
Teringson, James, 2
Terrington, Charles, 35
Tetston (?), Jeremiah, 41
Tew, Alen, 38

Tew, Jonathan, 38
Tew, Petter, 38
Tew, Walter, 39
Tharp, see Sharp
Tharp, Charnick, 32
Tharp, Elizabeth, 41
Tharp, W. A., 3
Tharp, Wm., 43
Thernin(?), John, 42
Thigpen, Joseph, 32
Thomas, D. K., 14
Thomas, Eliot, 17
Thomas, Emanuel, 38
Thomas, Hamton, 11
Thomas, James, 33
Thomas, Joel, 38
Thomas, John, 10
Thomas, Josiah, 2
Thomas, Morton, 7
Thomas, Moses, 50
Thomas, Samuel, 33
Thomas, T. H., 2
Thomas, Wm., 40, 51
Thomas, Zachariah, 14
Thompson, Hilman, 16
Thompson, Wm., 37
Tiler, James, 52
Tiller, Martain, 45
Tilman, Robert, 46
Tindal, John, 14
Titwell, James, 53
Titwell, Willey, 51
Tober, S., 31
Tolston, Henry, 43
Tompkins, Bill J., 21
Tompkins, H. M., 54
Torrence, A. R., 53
Trainum, G. W., 51
Tramel, J. J., 52
Trawick, James, 48
Treadwell, A., 30
Tryon, W. M., 25
Tucker, James, 50
Tully, J. R., 27
Turner, D. F., 35
Turner, N. W., 28

Underwood, C. W., 2
Utsey, Jacob, 8

Valentine, J., 41
Valentine, Lewis, 6
Valentine, Mathew, 11
Vann, John, 7
Vann, Leonard, 21